The Twin Flame Handbook
By
J. Brownbridge

For T.

INTRODUCTION

Welcome to the twin flame handbook. This Book is designed to provide guidance and support for those embarking on the transformative journey of the dark night of the soul within the context of a twin flame connection. We will explore the initial meeting, the escalation of the journey, the importance of shadow work, and ultimately, how to let go and move forward on your spiritual path.

The twin flame journey has been pretty gruelling for me personally. I hope this book can help you navigate your journey and help you do what may feel impossible...let go of the outcome. Only then can you feel whole again. With or without them.

CHAPTER 1

UNDERSTANDING TWIN FLAMES

THE DIVINE UNION

SOUL RECOGNITION

Exploring the deep sense of familiarity and recognition experienced upon meeting your twin flame, often described as a remembrance of an eternal connection. Soul recognition refers to the deep and profound connection that occurs when two souls who are part of the same "soul family" or "soul group" encounter each other. Twin flames are believed to be two halves of the same soul that have split and taken separate physical forms.

Soul recognition goes beyond physical attraction or intellectual compatibility. It is an intense and immediate sense of familiarity and resonance that is felt at a soul level. When twin flames meet, there is often a strong magnetic pull, an unexplainable feeling of knowing each other on a deeper level, and a sense of coming home.

This recognition is not based on external appearances or superficial qualities but rather on a profound soul-level connection. It's as if the souls recognize each other and remember their shared journey and purpose. This recognition can be accompanied by a range of emotions, including love, excitement, and a sense of completeness.

MIRROR EFFECT

Understanding how twin flames serve as mirrors, reflecting both the light and shadow aspects of each other for soul growth and self-awareness.

The mirror effect refers to the dynamic that occurs when two individuals in a twin flame relationship reflect each other's strengths, weaknesses, and unresolved issues. It is believed that twin flames serve as mirrors for each other, reflecting back aspects of themselves that they need to work on or heal.

The mirror effect can manifest in various ways. For example, if one twin flame struggles with trust issues, the other twin flame may exhibit behaviours that trigger those trust issues, forcing the first twin flame to confront and resolve them. Similarly, if one twin flame has difficulty expressing their emotions, the other twin flame may exhibit emotional intensity, mirroring the need for emotional healing and expression.

This mirroring effect can be intense and often leads to emotional and spiritual growth for both individuals. It pushes them to face their own shadows, confront their fears, and heal past wounds. Through this process, they can achieve greater self-awareness, self-acceptance, and personal transformation.

It's important to note that the mirror effect can sometimes be challenging and uncomfortable, as it brings up deep-seated issues and triggers. However, it is considered an essential part of the twin flame journey, as it provides opportunities for both individuals to evolve and align with their true selves.

UNITY OF ESSENCE

Delving into the concept that twin flames are two halves of the same soul, experiencing duality and separation to facilitate spiritual evolution.

Unity of Essence refers to the belief that despite being two separate individuals, twin flames share a fundamental essence or core energy. It suggests that at their deepest level, twin flames are united and interconnected.

The concept of Unity of Essence implies that twin flames are not merely two separate souls, but rather two aspects of the same soul. They are believed to originate from a single source or soul energy, which then splits into two halves. Each half takes on its own physical form, embodying masculine, and feminine energies, and embarks on individual journeys in different lifetimes.

The Unity of Essence emphasizes the inseparable bond between twin flames. It suggests that even though they may be physically separated or experiencing different life paths, their souls remain eternally connected. They are thought to share a profound spiritual and energetic bond that transcends time and space. This understanding of Unity of Essence holds that the purpose of the twin flame journey is to experience personal growth, spiritual evolution, and reunion with the other half. It is believed that through various stages of personal development, healing, and transformation, twin flames eventually come back together in order to merge and reunite as one.

ONENESS IN SEPARATION

THE ILLUSION OF SEPARATION

Understanding that the physical and temporal separation experienced by twin flames is an illusion, as their souls remain eternally connected.

The illusion of separation refers to the perception or experience of being separate from one's twin flame, despite the underlying unity and interconnectedness between them. It is the belief that twin flames are separated or disconnected from each other, leading to a sense of longing, incompleteness, or loneliness.

The illusion of separation arises from the physical and earthly experience of twin flames being in separate bodies, living separate lives, and often being physically distant from each other. It can also stem from the challenges and obstacles that twin flames may encounter on their individual paths, such as timing, personal growth, or external circumstances.

This illusion of separation can be a source of deep emotional pain and longing for twin flames. It is believed to be a catalyst for their personal growth, as they are often driven to search for meaning, purpose, and ultimately, reunion with their other half. The illusion of separation serves as a spiritual journey, pushing twin flames to go beyond the physical realm and reconnect with the spiritual truth of their unity.

The ultimate goal of recognizing the illusion of separation is to transcend it and awaken to the inherent unity and connection that exists between twin flames. It involves recognizing that the perceived separation is temporary and illusory, and that at a deeper level, twin flames are always connected and part of the same energetic essence.

MULTIDIMENSIONAL EXPERIENCE

Exploring the idea that while twin flames may be experiencing individual lifetimes, their higher selves exist beyond time and space, simultaneously experiencing multiple realities.

Multidimensional experience refers to the belief that the connection between twin flames extends beyond the physical plane and encompasses various dimensions of existence. It suggests that twin flames have a profound spiritual connection that transcends time, space, and the limitations of the physical realm.

The concept of multidimensional experience recognizes that twin flame relationships involve interactions and connections on multiple levels of consciousness and reality. It suggests that twin flames can communicate and interact not only in the physical realm but also in the spiritual, energetic, and astral realms.

According to this belief, twin flames can have experiences that go beyond the ordinary human perception. They may have telepathic communication, where they can sense each other's thoughts or emotions without physical contact. They may also have shared dreams or astral encounters, where they meet and interact in the dream state or in the realm of the astral plane.

The multidimensional experience also acknowledges the role of higher realms and spiritual guidance in the twin flame journey. It is believed that twin flames are guided and supported by higher beings, spirit guides, or higher aspects of themselves in their quest for reunion and spiritual growth.

This concept of multidimensional experience emphasizes the expansive and transcendent nature of the twin flame connection. It suggests that the bond between twin flames extends far beyond the physical plane and encompasses a larger spiritual reality.

THE HIGHER SELF AND SOUL EVOLUTION

THE HIGHER SELF
Understanding the concept of the higher self as the expanded, multidimensional aspect of one's consciousness, which guides and orchestrates soul growth and reunification.

The higher self refers to the spiritual aspect of an individual that is connected to a higher or divine consciousness. It is the part of oneself that is in tune with higher wisdom, unconditional love, and spiritual truth.

In the twin flame journey, the higher self plays a significant role. It is believed that twin flames are two halves of the same soul that have separated to embark on individual journeys of growth and learning. The higher self represents the spiritual essence of each twin flame, which remains connected and in communication with the divine and each other.

The higher self is often associated with qualities such as intuition, inner guidance, and a sense of purpose. It is the part of oneself that is aligned with one's soul's purpose and seeks spiritual evolution and unity. The higher self serves as a source of wisdom and guidance, offering insights and nudges to support the twin flame journey.

The higher self is believed to orchestrate synchronicities, signs, and divine timing to guide the reunion and alignment of the twin flames. It acts as a guiding force, supporting the growth and transformation of each individual as they work towards their reunion and spiritual union.

Connecting with and aligning with one's higher self is often considered an essential part of the twin flame journey. It involves deepening one's spiritual connection, practicing self-reflection, and cultivating a relationship with one's inner wisdom and divine consciousness.

PARALLEL LIFETIMES

Exploring the notion that while twin flames may appear separate in physical lifetimes, their higher selves are engaged in parallel journeys of growth and expansion.

Parallel lifetimes refer to the belief that twin flames share a history of past lives where they have existed simultaneously across different timelines or dimensions. It suggests that their souls have had multiple incarnations and have had experiences together in various lifetimes.

The concept of parallel lifetimes suggests that twin flames have a deep soul connection that transcends individual lifetimes. It is believed that their souls choose to incarnate in different bodies and live separate lives, but their paths often intersect, and they play significant roles in each other's journeys across different lifetimes.

In these parallel lifetimes, twin flames may have experienced various types of relationships or connections, such as romantic partners, family members, or close friends. They may have had different roles and dynamics in each lifetime, but the underlying soul connection remains constant.

The idea of parallel lifetimes emphasizes the concept of soul growth, learning, and evolution through the experiences shared by twin flames over multiple incarnations. It is believed that these lifetimes offer opportunities for the twin flames to heal past wounds, resolve karmic patterns, and ultimately reunite and achieve spiritual union.

Exploring and understanding parallel lifetimes can provide insights into the deeper dynamics and patterns within the twin flame connection. It can offer a broader perspective on the challenges, lessons, and purpose of the twin flame journey.

SOUL CONTRACTS AND DIVINE TIMING

Discussing the role of soul contracts and divine timing in the twin flame journey, as orchestrated by the higher self to facilitate optimal growth and reunion.

Soul contracts refer to the belief that before incarnating into physical bodies, souls make agreements or contracts with each other to meet, interact, and play specific roles in each other's lives. These contracts are believed to be predestined and purposeful, aimed at facilitating growth, learning, and spiritual evolution for all parties involved.

It is believed that twin flames have made a soul contract to meet and experience a deep connection in their earthly journey. The contract may include specific lessons, challenges, and experiences that the twin flames agreed to encounter for their mutual growth and transformation.

Divine timing, on the other hand, refers to the idea that the timing of significant events and encounters in our lives is orchestrated by a higher divine intelligence or cosmic order. It suggests that certain events, including the reunion of twin flames, are not bound by human schedules or expectations but are divinely guided and timed for optimal spiritual growth and alignment.

Divine timing means that the reunion or coming together of twin flames is not solely dependent on the desires or efforts of the individuals involved. Instead, it is believed that the timing of their reunion is influenced by a higher divine plan, which takes into account the readiness, growth, and alignment of both twin flames on their individual paths.

The concept of soul contracts and divine timing highlights the spiritual nature of the twin flame journey. It suggests that there is a higher purpose and wisdom guiding the connection between twin flames, and that the timing of their reunion is intricately woven into their personal growth and soul evolution.

BEYOND TIME AND SPACE

THE ILLUSION OF LINEAR TIME
Exploring how time is a construct of the physical realm and how twin flames, as spiritual beings, can access and experience the timeless nature of their connection.
The illusion of linear time refers to the belief that time is not experienced as a linear progression but rather as a construct of our human perception. It suggests that in the spiritual realm, time is non-linear, and the concept of past, present, and future is fluid and interconnected.

For twin flames, the illusion of linear time is often associated with the idea that the reunion and fulfilment of the twin flame connection are not bound by conventional chronological time. It is believed that twin flames may experience a sense of timelessness, where the connection and love they share transcend the limitations of linear time.

From this perspective, the illusion of linear time means that the twin flame journey and the process of reunion may not unfold according to the expectations or timelines of the physical world. It is not uncommon for twin flames to experience delays, separations, or periods of apparent distance, only to find that these experiences were necessary for their individual growth and preparation for union.

The illusion of linear time also suggests that the twin flame connection exists beyond the physical plane. Twin flames are believed to share a deep soul connection that transcends time and space, and their souls may be simultaneously experiencing different lifetimes or dimensions.

This understanding challenges the notion that time is linear with fixed events. Instead, it invites twin flames to trust in the divine timing and surrender to the unfolding of their journey, knowing that their souls are connected regardless of the perceived passage of time.

QUANTUM ENTANGLEMENT

Discussing the concept of quantum entanglement and its relevance to the instantaneous communication and energetic connection between twin flames across distances.

Quantum entanglement refers to the belief that the souls of twin flames are energetically interconnected at a quantum level, regardless of physical distance or separation.

In quantum physics, entanglement refers to a phenomenon where two or more particles become correlated in such a way that the state of one particle is instantly related to the state of another, even if they are separated by large distances. Changes made to one particle's properties instantaneously affect the other particle, regardless of the spatial separation between them.

Quantum entanglement is extended to the spiritual and metaphysical realm. It suggests that the souls of twin flames are deeply interconnected, and any changes or experiences one twin flame undergoes can be felt by the other, regardless of physical proximity.

According to this belief, the bond between twin flames is not solely dependent on physical contact or communication but operates on a higher energetic level. It is believed that the souls of twin flames remain entangled, sharing a profound connection that transcends time, space, and physical limitations.

Quantum entanglement suggests that the experiences, emotions, and spiritual growth of one twin flame can impact the other, creating a resonance and energetic exchange between them. It is often associated with telepathic communication, empathic connections, and a deep sense of knowing or feeling what the other twin flame is experiencing.

UNITY IN THE ETERNAL NOW

Understanding that true union with a twin flame occurs in the present moment, where past, present, and future converge, transcending the limitations of time and space.
Unity in the eternal now refers to the belief that the ultimate state of the twin flame connection is a timeless and unified experience of love, consciousness, and spiritual oneness.

The concept of Unity in the Eternal Now suggests that twin flames are destined to reunite and merge at a soul level, transcending the limitations of time and space. It implies that the separation and challenges experienced on the earthly plane are temporary illusions, and the true essence of the twin flame connection exists in a timeless, eternal realm.

In this state of unity, twin flames are believed to experience a deep sense of interconnectedness, where their souls merge and become one. It is a state of complete harmony, love, and understanding, where there is no distinction between individual identities or separate consciousness. Twin flames are believed to merge their energies and become a unified whole.

The concept of Unity in the Eternal Now emphasizes the spiritual purpose of the twin flame journey, which is to rediscover and experience this profound state of unity and love. It suggests that the challenges, growth, and healing encountered on the twin flame path are all leading towards the ultimate reunion and realization of this unity.

THE INITIAL MEETING

SOUL RECOGNITION

Exploring the intense and immediate sense of familiarity, connection, and spiritual resonance experienced upon meeting your twin flame.

Soul recognition refers to the deep and profound sense of familiarity, resonance, and connection that occurs when two souls encounter each other. It is the innate knowing and recognition at a soul level that the other person is not just a stranger, but someone with whom there is a significant and extraordinary bond.

When twin flames meet, there is often a strong sense of familiarity, as if they have known each other before or have a deep history together. This recognition goes beyond physical appearance or personality traits and resonates at a deeper soul level. It is a recognition of the shared essence, energy, and purpose that exists between the twin flames.

Soul recognition can manifest in various ways, such as an instant and intense attraction, a feeling of coming home, a sense of completion, or a magnetic pull towards each other. It may also involve a deep sense of understanding, acceptance, and unconditional love.

This recognition often triggers a profound transformation and awakening within the individuals involved. It ignites a spiritual journey of self-discovery, healing, and personal growth. Twin flames are drawn to each other to support each other's spiritual evolution and to fulfil their shared purpose and mission.

UNEXPLAINABLE MAGNETISM

Understanding the inexplicable pull and attraction that surpasses mere physical or emotional chemistry.

Unexplainable magnetism refers to the intense and irresistible attraction that twin flames feel towards each other, often defying logical explanations or conventional understanding. It is a powerful and unexplainable pull that draws twin flames together, transcending physical, emotional, and intellectual factors.

This magnetism goes beyond the usual dynamics of attraction and chemistry. It is a profound energetic connection that exists between twin flames. It is a force that pulls them towards each other, even in the face of obstacles, challenges, or logical reasons to stay apart.

The unexplainable magnetism experienced between twin flames can manifest in various ways. It may be a strong physical and sexual attraction, a deep emotional bond, or a sense of spiritual resonance. It often involves a feeling of completion or a sense of finding something missing in oneself when in the presence of the other. This magnetism is often described as a soul-level recognition and alignment. It is believed to be a result of the energetic compatibility and the shared essence between twin flames. It is as if their souls are naturally drawn to each other, and no external factors can fully explain or replicate the depth of the connection.

The unexplainable magnetism can be both exhilarating and challenging for twin flames. It can trigger intense emotions and be the catalyst for spiritual growth and transformation necessary for their journey. But also, for self-discovery, healing, and the pursuit of higher spiritual truths.

SYNCHRONICITIES AND DIVINE TIMING

Discussing the presence of meaningful synchronicities and divine timing surrounding the initial meeting, indicating the significance of the connection.

Synchronicities and divine timing refer to the occurrence of meaningful coincidences and the notion that events unfold according to a higher divine plan or order.

Synchronicities are significant coincidences that hold personal meaning or significance to the individuals experiencing them. These events may appear as seemingly unrelated occurrences or events that are connected through their underlying symbolism or timing. Synchronicities are often regarded as signs or messages from the universe, guiding and validating the twin flame journey.

Synchronicities are believed to play a crucial role in the reunion and alignment of twin flames. They can serve as confirmation of the deep connection between twin flames and can provide guidance and reassurance along their journey. Synchronicities may include repeated number patterns, significant encounters, shared dreams, or other symbolic occurrences that hold personal meaning for the twin flames. Divine timing, on the other hand, refers to the belief that significant events and experiences unfold according to a higher divine plan or order. It suggests that there is a perfect timing and orchestration of events that are beyond human control or understanding. In the twin flame journey, divine timing implies that the reunion and union of twin flames are not solely determined by human desires or efforts but are guided and aligned with a higher spiritual purpose.

Divine timing is often associated with the idea that twin flames need to go through their individual growth, healing, and preparation before they can fully come together. It involves surrendering to the timing of the universe and trusting that everything unfolds in the most appropriate way and at the most opportune time. Synchronicities and divine timing work hand in hand in the twin flame journey. Synchronicities serve as signs and guidance along the path, while divine timing ensures that the reunion and alignment of twin flames occur when both individuals are ready for the deep spiritual union.

DISTINGUISHING TWIN FLAMES FROM KARMIC CONNECTIONS

DEPTH OF CONNECTION

Exploring the profound and all-encompassing nature of the twin flame connection, which often goes beyond the surface-level dynamics of a karmic relationship.

Depth of connection refers to the profound and intense level of connection that exists between twin flames at a soul level. It goes beyond superficial or surface-level connections and encompasses a deep understanding, resonance, and bond between the two individuals.

The depth of connection experienced by twin flames is often described as a feeling of being seen, known, and understood on a profound level. It is a connection that transcends physical attraction or intellectual compatibility and delves into the core essence of each individual.

This depth of connection can manifest in various ways. It may involve a deep emotional bond where twin flames can share their deepest vulnerabilities, fears, and dreams with each other. It may also involve a spiritual resonance where twin flames feel a sense of alignment and shared purpose in their spiritual journeys.

The depth of connection between twin flames often involves a high degree of empathy and telepathic communication. Twin flames can often sense each other's emotions, thoughts, and energies, even when physically separated. There is a sense of being interconnected and intertwined at a soul level.

This depth of connection can be both beautiful and challenging for twin flames. It can bring immense joy, love, and growth, but it can also trigger deep healing, transformation, and the surfacing of unresolved wounds. Twin flames are often drawn together to support each other's healing and growth, as the depth of their connection can illuminate areas that require attention and transformation.

CATALYST FOR GROWTH

Understanding how the twin flame journey serves as a catalyst for profound personal and spiritual growth, while karmic connections may focus more on resolving specific karmic lessons.
Catalyst for growth refers to the role that the twin flame connection plays in triggering personal and spiritual growth in each individual. The twin flame relationship often serves as a catalyst, propelling individuals to embark on a transformative journey of self-discovery, healing, and inner growth.
The intense and unique dynamics of the twin flame connection can bring to the surface unresolved emotional wounds,

patterns, and issues that need to be addressed and healed. The presence of the twin flame acts as a mirror, reflecting back aspects of oneself that require attention and transformation.

The twin flame connection often stirs up deep emotions, challenges existing belief systems, and pushes individuals out of their comfort zones. This can lead to profound inner work and growth as individuals confront their fears, insecurities, and limitations.

The twin flame journey encourages self-reflection, self-awareness, and personal development. It invites individuals to examine their patterns of behaviour, belief systems, and emotional wounds. It pushes them to confront their shadow aspects and make conscious choices for their growth and well-being.

While the twin flame connection can be intense and challenging, it also offers immense opportunities for healing and transformation. The growth that occurs through the twin flame journey is often transformative and leads to greater self-love, self-acceptance, and spiritual evolution.

It's important to note that the twin flame journey is not solely focused on the reunion or romantic aspects of the relationship but emphasizes the individual growth and spiritual development of each person. The challenges and growth opportunities presented in the twin flame connection are meant to help individuals evolve and align with their higher selves.

INTENSE MIRROR EFFECT

Exploring how twin flames act as mirrors, reflecting both the light and shadow aspects of each other, often triggering deep emotional responses, and encouraging inner healing and growth. The intense mirror effect refers to the phenomenon where the twin flame relationship acts as a powerful mirror, reflecting back aspects of oneself, both light and shadow, for the purpose of self-awareness, growth, and transformation. When twin flames come together, their connection often triggers a deep reflection of one another. They serve as mirrors, reflecting each other's strengths, weaknesses, patterns, and unresolved issues. This mirror effect can be intense and challenging as it brings to light aspects of oneself that may have been hidden or overlooked.

The intense mirror effect allows twin flames to see themselves more clearly, often through the reflection of their counterpart. It can bring awareness to patterns, wounds, and beliefs that need healing and transformation. Twin flames may find themselves confronted with their deepest fears, insecurities, and unresolved emotional baggage through their interactions with each other.

This mirror effect is not limited to the challenging aspects but also reflects the positive qualities and potential within each twin flame. It helps them recognize and embody their strengths, gifts, and highest potential. Twin flames can inspire each other to grow, evolve, and step into their authentic selves.

The intense mirror effect can lead to a deep process of self-reflection and self-discovery. It invites twin flames to take responsibility for their own growth and healing, as they recognize that the change they seek in the relationship begins within themselves. It requires a willingness to face one's own shadows, confront inner wounds, and make conscious choices for personal transformation.

While the mirror effect can be confronting and emotionally intense, it is ultimately a catalyst for personal growth, healing, and self-empowerment. It supports the twin flame journey of self-realization, self-love, and spiritual evolution.

UNCONDITIONAL LOVE AND ACCEPTANCE

Discussing the overwhelming sense of acceptance, understanding, and unconditional love that characterizes the twin flame connection.

Unconditional love and acceptance refer to the deep and unwavering love and acceptance that twin flames have for each other, regardless of their flaws, past experiences, or challenges.

Twin flames are believed to share a profound connection rooted in love at a soul level. Unconditional love in the twin flame relationship means loving the other person without conditions or expectations. It is a love that transcends the ego and embraces the entirety of the other person, including their strengths, weaknesses, and imperfections.

In the twin flame journey, unconditional love and acceptance involve seeing the other person for who they truly are, beyond surface-level attributes or past mistakes. It means acknowledging and embracing the totality of their being, including their light and shadow aspects.

Unconditional love and acceptance also extend to the self. Twin flames are encouraged to practice self-love and self-acceptance as they navigate their individual healing and growth. This includes accepting and loving oneself fully, with all strengths and vulnerabilities.

Unconditional love and acceptance in the twin flame connection create a safe and nurturing space for both individuals to grow, heal, and evolve. It allows them to support each other through challenges and provide a compassionate presence for each other's journey.

It's important to note that unconditional love and acceptance does not mean tolerating harmful or toxic behaviour. It means loving and accepting the essence of the other person while also setting healthy boundaries and promoting growth and well-being.

Unconditional love and acceptance are spiritual concepts that emphasize the importance of love, compassion, and understanding in the twin flame journey. They are qualities that twin flames strive to embody as they navigate the complexities and transformations of their connection.

DIVINE PURPOSE AND ALIGNMENT

Recognizing the shared sense of purpose, mission, or calling that often emerges within the twin flame relationship, signifying a deeper spiritual alignment.
Divine purpose and alignment refer to the belief that the twin flame connection serves a higher spiritual purpose and that the reunion and journey of twin flames are guided by a divine plan or order.

Twin flames are believed to come together for a significant reason beyond a conventional romantic relationship. They are thought to have a shared mission or purpose that involves spiritual growth, service, and contributing to the greater good.

Divine purpose in the twin flame journey often relates to personal and collective healing, transformation, and spiritual evolution. The union of twin flames is seen as a catalyst for their individual and mutual growth, as well as for the expansion of consciousness on a larger scale.

Alignment with divine purpose entails being attuned to and aligned with the higher guidance and wisdom that flows through the twin flame connection. It involves listening to one's intuition, following one's heart, and surrendering to the divine flow of life.

Divine purpose and alignment also imply being in alignment with one's own soul's purpose and authentic self. It involves discovering and living in accordance with one's true nature, gifts, and passions.

The journey of twin flames often involves navigating obstacles, challenges, and inner transformation to align with their divine purpose. It requires embracing personal growth, healing, and self-discovery, while also recognizing the interconnectedness of their purpose with that of their counterpart.

Divine purpose and alignment provide a sense of meaning, direction, and fulfilment in the twin flame journey. They serve as a compass guiding twin flames towards their highest potentials and supporting their shared mission.

NAVIGATING THE CONNECTION.

EMOTIONAL TURBULENCE AND GROWTH

Understanding that the twin flame journey is not always smooth, often involving emotional challenges, conflicts, and intense inner work. These difficulties serve as opportunities for profound growth and transformation.

Emotional turbulence and growth refer to the intense emotional experiences and challenges that arise within the twin flame relationship, which ultimately lead to personal growth and transformation.

The twin flame connection often stirs up deep emotions and triggers unresolved wounds, fears, and insecurities in both individuals. This emotional turbulence can manifest as heightened emotional intensity, mood swings, and a rollercoaster of feelings.

The emotional turbulence experienced in the twin flame relationship is a result of the profound soul-level connection between twin flames. It serves as a catalyst for healing and growth, as it brings to the surface unresolved emotional issues that need to be addressed and transformed. Twin flames often find themselves navigating intense emotional states such as love, joy, passion, but also fear, anger, and sadness. The strong emotional charge in the relationship can be both exhilarating and challenging. It pushes twin flames to confront their deepest emotions, patterns, and belief systems.

However, within the emotional turbulence, there is also great potential for growth. Twin flames are invited to dive into their emotional landscapes, embrace vulnerability, and engage in deep self-reflection. They learn to acknowledge and process their emotions, heal past wounds, and develop greater emotional maturity and resilience.

The emotional turbulence experienced in the twin flame journey allows individuals to develop a deeper understanding of themselves, their triggers, and their emotional patterns. It supports the process of inner healing and fosters greater self-awareness, self-compassion, and emotional intelligence.

Through this emotional turbulence, twin flames have the opportunity to grow individually and together. They learn to navigate challenging emotions with love and understanding, and to hold space for each other's emotional journeys. The growth that emerges from this process often leads to increased emotional balance, harmony, and a deeper capacity for love and empathy.

It's important to note that the emotional turbulence and growth are subjective experiences and may vary for each individual and couple. The journey is highly personal, and the emotional challenges and growth opportunities may differ in each unique twin flame connection.

ENERGETIC BOND AND TELEPATHIC COMMUNICATION

Exploring the intense energetic bond and the ability to communicate telepathically, even during physical separation.

An energetic bond refers to the profound connection and exchange of energy between twin flames at a soul level. It goes beyond physical and emotional connection and encompasses a deep energetic resonance and unity.

The energetic bond between twin flames is believed to be established and sustained by the energetic and spiritual aspects of their beings. It is a connection that transcends time, space, and physical limitations. Twin flames often experience a sense of being energetically connected, even when physically separated.

Telepathic communication is a significant aspect of the energetic bond between twin flames. It is the ability to communicate and exchange information without the need for verbal or physical cues. Twin flames often report a strong telepathic connection, where they can intuitively sense each other's thoughts, emotions, and energies. This telepathic communication can occur through various means, such as receiving sudden insights, hearing the other person's voice in their mind, or feeling a strong intuitive knowing. It is a form of communication that transcends the limitations of ordinary senses and relies on the energetic connection between twin flames.

The energetic bond and telepathic communication in the twin flame connection facilitate a deep understanding and connection between the two individuals. It allows them to feel and experience each other's presence on a profound level, even when physically apart. It can bring a sense of comfort, support, and guidance as twin flames navigate their journey.

The energetic bond and telepathic communication also play a role in the mutual growth and healing of twin flames. Through their energetic connection, twin flames can support each other's transformation and facilitate the release of energetic blockages and unresolved emotions.

UNYIELDING PULL AND UNSHAKEABLE CONNECTION

Recognizing the unwavering connection and the inability to fully let go, despite challenges or periods of separation.

The terms "unyielding pull" and "unshakeable connection" refer to the powerful and undeniable attraction and bond that exists between twin flames.

These terms describe the deep and magnetic connection that draws twin flames towards each other and sustains their relationship.

The unyielding pull represents the intense gravitational force that twin flames experience towards one another. It is often described as a strong, irresistible, and magnetic attraction that transcends physical and logical explanations. Twin flames may feel an inexplicable and undeniable longing to be in each other's presence, to connect, and to unite.

This unyielding pull goes beyond romantic or superficial attraction. It is a profound soul-level connection that draws twin flames together to fulfil their shared purpose, learn valuable lessons, and support each other's growth and evolution.

The unshakeable connection refers to the enduring and unwavering bond between twin flames. It is a connection that remains steadfast and strong, even in the face of challenges, separation, or external circumstances. Twin flames may go through periods of physical or emotional distance, but the unshakeable connection remains intact.

This unshakeable connection is often described as a deep knowing and recognition of the other person's essence and soul. Twin flames may feel an innate sense of familiarity, as if they have known each other for eternity. It creates a sense of security, trust, and stability in the relationship, even during turbulent times. The unyielding pull and unshakeable connection are believed to be the result of the unique energetic and spiritual bond that twin flames share. It is a connection that transcends ordinary relationships and defies conventional explanations.

TRUSTING YOUR INNER KNOWING

INTUITION AND INNER GUIDANCE
Encouraging individuals to trust their intuition and inner knowing when discerning whether they are on a twin flame journey or in a karmic relationship.
Intuition and inner guidance refer to the heightened sense of intuition and inner knowing that twin flames often experience in their relationship and personal journeys. Intuition is the ability to receive insights, information, and guidance beyond the scope of rational thinking or sensory perception. It is a deep inner knowing that comes from a place of inner wisdom and connection to higher realms of consciousness.

Twin flames frequently report a strong sense of intuition in their interactions with their counterpart. They may have a heightened ability to sense the emotions, thoughts, and needs of their twin flame without explicit communication. This intuitive understanding can extend to various aspects of the twin flame journey, including the timing of reunions, decisions, and the overall direction of their connection.

Inner guidance, on the other hand, is the internal compass or wisdom that guides twin flames on their individual paths of growth and evolution. It is the inner voice, feelings, or impulses that provide insights, clarity, and direction.

Twin flames often rely on their inner guidance to navigate the complexities and challenges of their relationship. This inner guidance can help them make decisions that align with their highest good, facilitate healing and self-discovery, and support their overall spiritual journey.

Intuition and inner guidance play an essential role in the twin flame connection as they foster deeper self-awareness, trust, and alignment with one's soul's purpose. By listening to their intuition and following their inner guidance, twin flames can make choices and take actions that are in alignment with their authentic selves and the evolution of their connection.

It's important to note that intuition and inner guidance are subjective experiences and may vary for each individual and twin flame couple. The level of sensitivity to intuition and the way inner guidance is received can differ from person to person.

SELF-REFLECTION AND DISCERNMENT

Emphasizing the importance of self-reflection, discernment, and deep inner work to gain clarity about the nature of the connection.

Self-reflection and discernment refer to the processes of introspection, self-examination, and the ability to make discerning judgments and choices in the twin flame journey.

Self-reflection involves turning inward and examining one's thoughts, feelings, beliefs, and behaviours in relation to the twin flame connection. It is a practice of deep self-awareness and introspection, where individuals take the time to reflect on their own patterns, triggers, and areas of growth. Twin flame relationships often bring to the surface unresolved issues, past traumas, and patterns that require healing and transformation. Self-reflection allows individuals to explore and understand their own contributions to the dynamics of the relationship. It helps them identify areas where personal growth and healing are needed, allowing for greater self-awareness and self-empowerment.

Discernment, on the other hand, refers to the ability to make wise and careful judgments and choices. It involves the skill of distinguishing between different options, perspectives, and energies, and making decisions that align with one's highest good and soul's evolution.

Discernment in the twin flame journey is particularly important due to the intense emotions and challenges that may arise. It requires individuals to tune into their inner guidance, intuition, and higher wisdom to make choices that promote their personal growth, well-being, and alignment with their authentic selves.

Self-reflection and discernment go hand in hand. By engaging in self-reflection, twin flames gain a deeper understanding of themselves and their patterns, which enhances their ability to discern what is truly beneficial for their growth and the growth of their connection.

These practices help twin flames cultivate a sense of self-responsibility and personal empowerment. They encourage individuals to take ownership of their own healing, growth, and choices, rather than relying solely on external validation or expectations.

Self-reflection and discernment are ongoing processes in the twin flame journey, as individuals continuously learn, evolve, and make choices aligned with their own truth and higher purpose. They foster personal development, self-mastery, and the ability to create a balanced and harmonious connection with their twin flame.

It's important to note that self-reflection and discernment are subjective experiences and may vary for each individual and twin flame couple. The extent and depth of self-reflection and the discernment process can differ based on personal circumstances and the stage of the twin flame journey.

Self-reflection and discernment align with the belief that personal growth and self-awareness are integral to the twin flame journey and contribute to the overall evolution of the connection.

DIVINE CONFIRMATION

Acknowledging that external signs, synchronicities, and messages from the universe can also provide confirmation and validation of the twin flame journey.
Divine confirmation refers to the signs, synchronicities, and messages that are believed to be messages from the divine or higher realms that validate and affirm the twin flame connection.

When twin flames embark on their journey, they often experience a series of meaningful and synchronistic events that seem to be beyond mere coincidence. These events serve as confirmation from the divine or higher powers that they are on

the right path and that their connection is
divinely guided.

Divine confirmation can manifest in various
ways, such as repeated number patterns
(e.g., 1111, 222, 333), meaningful symbols
or signs appearing in everyday life, or
serendipitous encounters. These
occurrences may provide twin flames with a
sense of reassurance, encouragement, or
guidance.

Furthermore, twin flames may receive
intuitive insights, inner knowing, or
messages from their higher selves, spirit
guides, or the universe that confirm the
significance and purpose of their
connection. These messages may come
through dreams, meditation, or other
spiritual practices, offering guidance, clarity,
or support in their twin flame journey.

Divine confirmation plays a crucial role in
the twin flame journey, as it strengthens

the faith and belief in the deeper spiritual aspects of the connection. It helps twin flames stay committed and resilient during challenging times, knowing that their union is divinely ordained and part of a greater plan.

It's important to note that the interpretation of divine confirmation is subjective and personal to each individual or twin flame couple. What may be perceived as a sign or confirmation by one person may hold different significance or meaning for another. It is essential for twin flames to trust their intuition and inner guidance when discerning the messages and signs they receive.

By exploring these aspects, we can gain a deeper understanding of the initial meeting with a twin flame and how to discern whether it is a true twin flame connection or a karmic relationship. Remember that each journey is unique, and the key lies in trusting your inner guidance, navigating the challenges with love and growth, and embracing the profound transformation that the twin flame journey offers.

CHAPTER 2

THE DARK NIGHT OF THE SOUL UNVEILED

RECOGNIZING THE DARK NIGHT

Understanding the signs and symptoms of the dark night of the soul within a twin flame relationship.

Recognizing the Dark Night refers to the stage or period of intense emotional and spiritual turmoil that twin flames may experience during their journey of self-discovery and union.

The Dark Night is often described as a period of deep inner healing and transformation. It is characterized by intense emotional challenges, such as feelings of loneliness, confusion, fear, despair, and facing unresolved wounds and traumas. It can be a time of intense purging and releasing of old patterns, beliefs, and attachments that no longer serve the growth and evolution of the individual or the twin flame connection.

During this stage, twin flames may confront their deepest fears, insecurities, and shadow aspects. It is a time of confronting and healing deep-seated emotional wounds, conditioning, and past traumas that may have been buried or repressed. The Dark Night pushes twin flames to face their inner demons, enabling them to grow, evolve, and ultimately heal.

While the Dark Night can be a challenging and painful experience, it serves a crucial purpose in the twin flame journey. It provides an opportunity for profound self-reflection, introspection, and self-awareness. It helps twin flames shed old layers of conditioning and illusions, making space for their authentic selves to emerge. Recognizing the Dark Night requires twin flames to be willing to confront their inner struggles and embrace the process of healing and growth. It is a time of surrender, trust, and faith in the transformative power of the journey.

It's important to note that the Dark Night is not a fixed or linear stage in the twin flame journey, and its duration can vary for each individual or twin flame couple. Some may experience shorter periods of intensity, while others may go through more prolonged and challenging phases.

The concept of the Dark Night draws inspiration from spiritual and psychological teachings, particularly the works of mystics such as St. John of the Cross. It acknowledges that the path to union and self-realization often involves navigating through the darkness to emerge into the light.

While the Dark Night can be a difficult and tumultuous phase, it is seen as an essential part of the twin flame journey, as it allows individuals to heal, grow, and ultimately reunite with their true selves and their twin flame in a more authentic and profound way.

STAGES OF ESCALATION

Exploring how the dark night intensifies within the twin flame journey and the challenges faced at each stage.
The stages of escalation refer to the various phases or levels of intensity and growth that twin flame relationships can go through. These stages are often characterized by increasing levels of challenge, emotional intensity, and spiritual transformation.
It's important to note that the specific stages and their order may vary among different sources and interpretations.

However, here is a general outline of the stages commonly associated with twin flame relationships:

1. Recognition and Awakening: This is the initial stage where twin flames recognize each other at a deep soul level. There is a sense of familiarity and a powerful connection that may trigger a spiritual awakening in both individuals.

2. Twin Flame Union: In this stage, twin flames come together and enter into a romantic or intimate relationship. The union can be intense, passionate, and transformative, as both individuals experience deep emotional and spiritual growth through the connection.

3. Turbulence and Purging: This stage often involves a period of intense emotional turmoil, challenges, and triggers. Old wounds, insecurities, and unresolved issues come to the surface, leading to a process of

purging and healing. It can be a time of significant growth and transformation for both individuals.

4. Separation and Runner-Chaser Dynamics: This stage is marked by physical or emotional separation, where one or both twin flames may pull away or experience resistance to the intensity of the connection. It can involve a push-pull dynamic, with one twin flame assuming the role of the "runner" and the other as the "chaser." This stage serves as an opportunity for individual growth, self-reflection, and healing.

5. Surrender and Healing: In this stage, twin flames begin to surrender to the journey and focus on their own healing and self-improvement. They learn to let go of attachment, control, and expectations, embracing the process of self-love and self-discovery. It is a time of

inner healing, acceptance, and personal growth.

6. Reunion and Harmonization: This stage involves the eventual reunion and harmonization of the twin flames. It may happen after a period of separation and individual growth. The reunion is often marked by a deep sense of inner peace, balance, and mutual understanding. Twin flames come together in a more harmonious and balanced union, supporting each other's spiritual journey and shared purpose.

It's important to remember that these stages are not necessarily linear or fixed. Twin flame relationships can go through cycles, and individuals may revisit certain stages multiple times as they continue to evolve and deepen their connection. These stages of escalation provide a framework to understand the common patterns and dynamics that often occur in these relationships. However, it's essential to approach the twin flame journey with an open mind and allow for the uniqueness and individuality of each relationship.

SPIRITUAL GROWTH AND PURIFICATION

Embracing the transformative opportunities and soul growth that emerge during the dark night.
Spiritual growth and purification refer to the process of inner transformation, healing, and the development of spiritual awareness that occurs throughout the twin flame journey.

Twin flame relationships are often seen as catalysts for spiritual growth and evolution. The intense connection and deep soul bond between twin flames provide opportunities for individuals to confront their inner wounds, limitations, and patterns. This process of self-reflection and self-discovery leads to spiritual growth and purification. Spiritual growth involves expanding one's consciousness, deepening their connection to their higher self or divine essence, and aligning with their true nature. It is a journey of self-realization, self-mastery, and self-transcendence. Through the twin flame connection, individuals are pushed to explore their spirituality, embrace their gifts, and awaken their spiritual potential. Purification, on the other hand, refers to the process of releasing and clearing old energies, beliefs, and patterns that no longer serve the highest good. It involves letting go of attachments, expectations, and ego-driven desires. Twin flame relationships often bring to the surface unresolved issues, emotional wounds, and past traumas, which require healing and purification.

The spiritual growth and purification in the twin flame journey involve:

1. Self-Reflection: Twin flames are encouraged to deeply reflect on themselves, their beliefs, and their patterns. They explore their shadows, confront their fears, and gain self-awareness.

2. Healing and Integration: Twin flames engage in inner healing work to address emotional wounds and traumas. This healing process involves forgiveness, self-compassion, and the integration of all aspects of the self.

3. Awakening and Self-Realization: The intense connection between twin flames often triggers spiritual awakenings. They become more aware of their divine nature, purpose, and the interconnectedness of all things.

4. Spiritual Practices: Twin flames often engage in spiritual practices

such as meditation, energy work, journaling, or connecting with higher realms. These practices support their spiritual growth, purification, and alignment with their authentic selves.

5. Surrender and Trust: Twin flames learn to surrender control and trust in the divine timing and guidance of their journey. They let go of the need to force outcomes and surrender to the flow of their connection and the lessons it brings.

Spiritual growth and purification are deeply personal and individualized. Each twin flame journey is unique, and the specific experiences and transformations may vary. The focus is on the expansion of consciousness, the integration of mind, body, and spirit, and the alignment with higher truths and purposes.

It's important to approach spiritual growth and purification in the twin flame journey with openness, patience, and self-compassion. It is a lifelong process that unfolds organically and requires dedication, self-reflection, and a willingness to embrace the transformative power of the journey.

RECOGNIZING THE DARK NIGHT

Recognizing the Dark Night of the Soul can be a deeply personal and subjective experience. However, there are several common signs and indicators that can help you recognize the onset of the Dark Night. Here are some ways to recognize this transformative phase:

1. Intense Emotional Turmoil: The Dark Night often brings forth intense

emotional upheaval, such as feelings of deep sadness, despair, loneliness, and confusion. You may find yourself questioning your path, your purpose, and even your connection with your twin flame.

2. Spiritual Emptiness and Disconnection: During the Dark Night, you may experience a sense of spiritual emptiness and disconnection. It may feel as if you have lost touch with your spiritual practices, beliefs, or the divine presence. There can be a profound longing for a deeper spiritual connection.

3. Energetic Shifts and Unsettling Experiences: You might encounter intense energetic shifts, such as heightened sensitivity, unusual dreams, synchronicities, or a sense of being spiritually tested. These experiences can feel unsettling and disruptive to your daily life.

4. Questioning the Twin Flame Connection: The Dark Night often brings a period of doubt and questioning about the nature of your twin flame connection. You might wonder if the journey is worth the challenges or if you are on the right path. This questioning is part of the deep inner work required during this phase.

5. Confronting Shadow Aspects: The Dark Night compels you to confront and heal your shadow aspects—the unresolved wounds, traumas, and negative patterns within yourself. This process can be uncomfortable and may involve facing difficult emotions, memories, and self-limiting beliefs.

6. Feeling Spiritually and Emotionally Stagnant: You may experience a sense of stagnation in your spiritual and emotional growth. It can feel as if you are at a standstill or facing a

blockage in your personal development. This stagnant phase is often a prelude to significant breakthroughs and transformation.

7. Longing for Union and Resolution: Despite the challenges and doubts, there is a deep longing for union, resolution, and spiritual growth. The intensity of this desire serves as a driving force to navigate the Dark Night and emerge stronger and more aligned with your true self.

It's important to note that these signs may vary in intensity and duration for different individuals. If you resonate with several of these indicators and feel that you are going through a profound inner transformation, it is likely that you are experiencing the Dark Night of the Soul within your twin flame journey.

Remember, the Dark Night is an opportunity for profound growth, healing, and spiritual evolution. Embrace the process with self-compassion, seek support from spiritual resources or trusted individuals, and engage in practices that promote self-care, self-reflection, and inner healing.

THE STAGES OF ESCALATION

The stages of escalation within the Dark Night of the Soul, specifically within the twin flame journey, involve a deepening intensity of the challenges and transformative experiences. While the exact progression and duration of each stage can vary among individuals, the following stages provide a general framework:

1. Awakening: The Awakening stage marks the initial recognition of the twin flame connection and the

spiritual journey that lies ahead. During this stage, there is a growing awareness of the deep soul bond and a longing for a deeper connection with the divine. It may be accompanied by a sense of excitement, fascination, and a desire to explore the depths of the relationship.

2. Turbulence and Conflict: As the twin flame journey progresses, conflicts and challenges arise, often triggering intense emotions and deep-rooted wounds. This stage is characterized by emotional turbulence, disagreements, and external or internal obstacles that test the strength of the connection. The purpose of this stage is to bring to the surface unresolved issues, patterns, and triggers that need to be addressed and healed for personal and collective growth.

3. Separation and Surrender: The Separation and Surrender stage involves physical or energetic distance between twin flames. It can be a profoundly painful and challenging stage where the connection may appear strained or even broken. This separation serves as an opportunity for individual growth, healing, and self-discovery. Surrendering attachment to the outcome and focusing on personal development become key aspects during this stage.

4. Healing and Integration: In the Healing and Integration stage, both twin flames embark on a deep inner healing process. This stage involves confronting and healing their own wounds, traumas, and limiting beliefs. The focus shifts to self-reflection, self-care, and self-love, as both individuals work on integrating

their shadow aspects and aligning with their authentic selves.

5. Union and Harmonization: The Union and Harmonization stage represents a deeper level of integration and alignment between twin flames. This stage is marked by a renewed connection, often on a higher energetic and spiritual level. It involves a harmonization of energies, a deepening understanding of the soul bond, and a shared commitment to personal growth and spiritual evolution.

It is important to note that these stages are not necessarily linear and can overlap or repeat. Each stage presents its unique challenges and opportunities for growth. It is crucial to approach the journey with patience, self-compassion, and a willingness to engage in deep inner work.

Remember, the ultimate purpose of the stages of escalation within the Dark Night of the Soul is to facilitate profound transformation, healing, and spiritual evolution for both individuals, leading to a more harmonious and aligned connection on a soul level.

SPIRITUAL GROWTH AND PURIFICATION

Spiritual growth and purification are fundamental aspects of the Dark Night of the Soul and the twin flame journey. They involve a deep inner transformation and alignment with one's true essence. Here are some key elements related to spiritual growth and purification:

1. Self-Reflection and Self-Awareness: Spiritual growth begins with self-

reflection and self-awareness. It involves examining your thoughts, emotions, beliefs, and behaviours to gain insight into your patterns, triggers, and areas for growth. Through self-reflection, you can identify areas that require healing and purification.

2. Shadow Work and Inner Healing: Shadow work is an integral part of the purification process. It involves diving into the depths of your unconscious mind and exploring the aspects of yourself that you have disowned or rejected. By facing and integrating your shadow aspects, you can heal wounds, release old traumas, and transform self-limiting beliefs.

3. Cultivating Mindfulness and Presence: Practicing mindfulness and being fully present in the present moment can support your spiritual growth and purification.

Mindfulness helps you observe your thoughts, emotions, and experiences without judgment, allowing you to develop a deeper understanding of yourself and the interconnected nature of existence.

4. Emotional Healing and Forgiveness: Emotional healing is crucial for spiritual growth and purification. It involves acknowledging and processing unresolved emotions, such as grief, anger, fear, or resentment. Through practices like forgiveness, compassion, and self-compassion, you can release emotional burdens and open your heart to greater love and acceptance.

5. Cultivating Virtues and Higher Qualities: Spiritual growth and purification involve cultivating virtues and higher qualities within yourself. This includes qualities such as love, compassion, forgiveness,

gratitude, humility, and authenticity. By embodying these qualities, you align with your higher self and contribute positively to your own growth and the world around you.

6. Connection with Higher Self and Divine: Developing a deeper connection with your higher self and the divine is a central aspect of spiritual growth and purification. This can be nurtured through practices like meditation, prayer, contemplation, or engaging in activities that bring you closer to your spiritual essence. Connecting with your higher self and the divine provides guidance, wisdom, and a sense of purpose.

7. Surrender and Trust: Spiritual growth and purification often require surrendering the need for control and trusting in the divine flow of life. Surrendering allows you to let go of attachments,

expectations, and resistance, enabling you to align with the greater wisdom and guidance of the universe.

Remember, spiritual growth and purification are ongoing processes. They require patience, commitment, and a willingness to engage in continuous self-reflection and inner work. Embrace the journey with an open heart, trust the process, and allow yourself to evolve and grow into your highest potential.

CHAPTER 3

SHADOW WORK AND SELF-EXPLORATION

UNDERSTANDING THE SHADOW

Shedding light on the concept of the shadow self and its significance within the twin flame journey.

Understanding the Shadow refers to the process of exploring and integrating the hidden, unconscious aspects of oneself. The shadow represents the parts of our personality, emotions, and beliefs that we have repressed, denied, or deemed unacceptable.

Twin flame relationships often bring these shadow aspects to the surface, as the intense connection and mirror effect between twin flames can trigger unresolved wounds, fears, and insecurities. By recognizing and understanding the shadow, twin flames can embark on a journey of self-discovery and healing, ultimately leading to personal growth and the evolution of the relationship.

Here are some key aspects of understanding the shadow:

1. Self-Awareness: Recognizing and acknowledging the presence of the shadow requires self-awareness. It involves observing one's thoughts, emotions, and behaviours without judgment and with a willingness to explore the deeper layers of the self.

2. Shadow Projection: Twin flame relationships often involve projecting aspects of the shadow onto each other. This can lead to intense conflicts, triggers, and challenges. By becoming aware of these projections, twin flames can gain insight into their own unresolved issues and take responsibility for their healing.

3. Integration and Acceptance: Understanding the shadow involves accepting and integrating the aspects of oneself that have been repressed or denied. It requires embracing all parts of oneself, including the perceived "negative" or "undesirable" qualities. Through self-acceptance, twin flames can cultivate compassion, understanding, and unconditional love for themselves and each other.

4. Healing and Transformation: Exploring the shadow allows twin

flames to heal past wounds and traumas. It involves facing fears, releasing old patterns, and transforming limiting beliefs. By shining light on the shadow aspects, twin flames can experience deep healing and personal transformation.

5. Balance and Wholeness: Understanding the shadow is a journey toward achieving balance and wholeness. It involves integrating the light and dark aspects of oneself, embracing both strengths and vulnerabilities. Twin flames strive to find a harmonious equilibrium within themselves and in their connection.

Understanding the shadow requires courage, self-reflection, and a willingness to delve into the depths of the self. It is a process of self-discovery and self-acceptance, allowing twin flames to embrace their authentic selves and foster a

more profound connection based on acceptance, compassion, and growth.
It's important to note that exploring the shadow is an ongoing process, and it may require the support of therapy, inner work, or spiritual practices. Each twin flame journey is unique, and the understanding of the shadow will vary for each individual and couple.

THE IMPORTANCE OF SHADOW WORK

Exploring the role of shadow work in healing past wounds, releasing patterns, and cultivating self-awareness.
Understanding the Shadow refers to the process of exploring and integrating the hidden, unconscious aspects of oneself. The shadow represents the parts of our personality, emotions, and beliefs that we have repressed, denied, or deemed unacceptable.

Twin flame relationships often bring these shadow aspects to the surface, as the intense connection and mirror effect between twin flames can trigger unresolved wounds, fears, and insecurities. By recognizing and understanding the shadow, twin flames can embark on a journey of self-discovery and healing, ultimately leading to personal growth and the evolution of the relationship.

Here are some key aspects of understanding the shadow:

1. Self-Awareness: Recognizing and acknowledging the presence of the shadow requires self-awareness. It involves observing one's thoughts, emotions, and behaviours without judgment and with a willingness to explore the deeper layers of the self.

2. Shadow Projection: Twin flame relationships often involve projecting aspects of the shadow onto each other. This can lead to intense conflicts, triggers, and

challenges. By becoming aware of these projections, twin flames can gain insight into their own unresolved issues and take responsibility for their healing.

3. Integration and Acceptance: Understanding the shadow involves accepting and integrating the aspects of oneself that have been repressed or denied. It requires embracing all parts of oneself, including the perceived "negative" or "undesirable" qualities. Through self-acceptance, twin flames can cultivate compassion, understanding, and unconditional love for themselves and each other.

4. Healing and Transformation: Exploring the shadow allows twin flames to heal past wounds and traumas. It involves facing fears, releasing old patterns, and transforming limiting beliefs. By shining light on the shadow aspects,

twin flames can experience deep healing and personal transformation.

5. Balance and Wholeness: Understanding the shadow is a journey toward achieving balance and wholeness. It involves integrating the light and dark aspects of oneself, embracing both strengths and vulnerabilities. Twin flames strive to find a harmonious equilibrium within themselves and in their connection.

Understanding the shadow requires courage, self-reflection, and a willingness to delve into the depths of the self. It is a process of self-discovery and self-acceptance, allowing twin flames to embrace their authentic selves and foster a more profound connection based on acceptance, compassion, and growth.

PRACTICAL TECHNIQUES

Providing effective strategies and exercises to engage in shadow work and navigate its challenges.

Engaging in shadow work can be a deeply personal and transformative journey. While the specific techniques and exercises may vary for each individual, here are some practical strategies that can support you in your shadow work process and help you navigate its challenges:

1. Self-Reflection and Journaling: Set aside regular time for self-reflection and journaling. Write about your thoughts, emotions, and experiences, allowing yourself to explore and express your inner world. Journaling can help you uncover patterns, triggers, and unconscious beliefs.

2. Meditation and Mindfulness: Practice meditation and mindfulness to cultivate present-moment awareness. This can help you observe your thoughts, emotions,

and bodily sensations without judgment. Mindfulness allows you to become more attuned to your shadow aspects as they arise.

3. Inner Child Work: Connect with your inner child and explore any unresolved wounds or traumas from your past. Visualizations, dialogues, or creative expression can assist in healing and integrating the wounded aspects of yourself.

4. Emotional Processing: Allow yourself to fully feel and express your emotions. Create a safe space for emotional processing through practices such as breathwork, movement, or artistic expression. Emotions often hold valuable information about your shadow aspects.

5. Shadow Dialogue: Engage in a dialogue with your shadow. You can do this through visualization or writing exercises. Ask questions,

listen to the responses, and engage in a compassionate conversation with your shadow aspects to gain understanding and insight.

6. Therapy or Counselling: Consider seeking support from a therapist or counsellor experienced in shadow work. A professional can guide and provide a safe space for deeper exploration and healing.

7. Shadow Integration Rituals: Design rituals or ceremonies that symbolize your commitment to integrating your shadow. This could involve writing down aspects of your shadow on paper and burning them as a symbolic release or creating a visual representation of your shadow and finding ways to honour and integrate it.

8. Self-Compassion and Self-Care: Be gentle and compassionate with yourself throughout the shadow work process. Practice self-care

activities that nourish your mind, body, and spirit. Taking care of yourself creates a supportive foundation for the deeper work.

9. Seek Guidance from Spiritual Teachers or Resources: Explore teachings and resources on shadow work from spiritual teachers, books, or online platforms. These can provide guidance, insights, and tools to assist you in your journey.

10. Patience and Perseverance: Embracing your shadow and integrating its aspects is an ongoing process. Be patient with yourself and the journey. Recognize that it takes time, effort, and commitment to delve into the depths of your psyche. Celebrate your progress and stay committed to your growth.

Remember, engaging in shadow work can bring up challenging emotions and aspects of yourself that may be uncomfortable to confront. Approach this work with self-compassion, and if you feel overwhelmed or stuck, consider seeking support from a professional or a community of like-minded individuals who can offer guidance and encouragement.

CHAPTER 4

LETTING GO AND MOVING FORWARD

SURRENDERING ATTACHMENTS
Understanding the necessity of releasing attachment to outcomes and expectations within the twin flame connection.
Surrendering refers to the process of letting go of expectations, desires, and dependencies that may hinder the growth and harmony of the twin flame connection. It involves releasing the need for control

and allowing the natural flow and evolution of the relationship to unfold.

Here are some key aspects of surrendering attachments:

1. Releasing Expectations: Surrendering attachments involves letting go of specific expectations about how the twin flame journey should unfold. It means allowing the connection to evolve in its own time and embracing the divine timing of the union. By releasing expectations, twin flames open themselves up to the limitless possibilities and lessons that the journey has to offer.

2. Detaching from Outcomes: Instead of fixating on a particular outcome or the idea of a perfect union, surrendering attachments involves focusing on inner growth and alignment with one's higher self. It means detaching from the need for the connection to fulfil specific external conditions or expectations.

This allows twin flames to surrender to the wisdom of the journey and trust that it is unfolding for their highest good.

3. Letting Go of Control: Surrendering attachments requires relinquishing the need for control over the twin flame connection. It means recognizing that each individual has their own path, lessons, and growth process. By letting go of control, twin flames create space for authenticity, individuality, and personal growth within the connection.

4. Embracing Divine Timing: Surrendering attachments involves embracing the concept of divine timing. It means trusting that the universe has a perfect plan and knowing that everything is unfolding in the right way and at the right time. Twin flames surrender to the natural progression of the

connection, allowing it to unfold according to the higher plan.

5. Cultivating Self-Love and Wholeness: Surrendering attachments also involves focusing on self-love and self-empowerment. Twin flames recognize that their happiness and fulfilment do not solely rely on the union with their counterpart. They invest in their own personal growth, healing, and well-being, finding wholeness within themselves rather than seeking it solely from the external connection.

6. Trusting the Journey: Surrendering attachments requires a deep trust in the twin flame journey. It involves surrendering to the ups and downs, the challenges, and lessons, and trusting that each experience is leading to growth and spiritual evolution. Trusting the journey allows twin flames to surrender to the divine guidance and wisdom

that is inherent within the connection.

Surrendering is a profound act of trust, faith, and self-empowerment. It allows twin flames to focus on their individual growth, align with their higher selves, and create a harmonious and balanced union. By surrendering attachments, twin flames open themselves up to the vast possibilities, lessons, and transformative power of the twin flame journey.

SELF-LOVE AND HEALING

Cultivating self-love and prioritizing personal healing to facilitate the journey forward.

Self-love and healing play a crucial role for twin flames. They refer to the process of nurturing and caring for oneself, as well as addressing and healing personal wounds and traumas. Here's a closer look at self-love and healing:

1. Self-Love: Self-love involves developing a deep and unconditional love and acceptance for oneself. It means recognizing one's inherent worthiness, embracing strengths and weaknesses, and practicing self-compassion. Self-love is essential because it allows individuals to establish a solid foundation of self-worth, which is vital for healthy and balanced relationships.

2. Inner Healing: Inner healing involves addressing and resolving past wounds, traumas, and unresolved emotional issues. It is a process of self-discovery, self-reflection, and self-care. Twin flame relationships

often bring to the surface deep-seated emotional wounds and triggers, and inner healing is necessary to release emotional baggage and promote personal growth.

3. Emotional Well-Being: Self-love and healing focus on nurturing emotional well-being. It involves developing emotional resilience, understanding one's emotions, and practicing emotional self-regulation. By prioritizing emotional well-being, twin flames can navigate the challenges of the relationship with greater clarity, stability, and emotional intelligence.

4. Boundaries and Self-Care: Self-love and healing involve setting healthy boundaries and practicing self-care. It means recognizing and honouring one's needs and priorities and taking proactive steps to meet them. Establishing boundaries ensures that

twin flames maintain a sense of self and individuality within the connection, while self-care nurtures physical, emotional, and spiritual well-being.

5. Forgiveness and Letting Go: Self-love and healing also encompass forgiveness and the willingness to let go of past hurts and grievances. Forgiveness is not about condoning harmful behaviour, but rather releasing the emotional burden and freeing oneself from resentment and bitterness. Letting go allows space for personal growth and the possibility of a renewed and healthier connection with the twin flame.

6. Self-Discovery and Personal Growth: Self-love and healing involve embracing self-discovery and personal growth. It means exploring one's passions, interests, and purpose, and actively working

towards personal development. By investing in self-growth, twin flames enhance their own well-being and contribute positively to the growth of the relationship.

7. Self-Reflection and Inner Work: Self-love and healing require consistent self-reflection and inner work. It involves examining one's beliefs, behaviours, and patterns, and taking responsibility for personal growth and transformation. Self-reflection and inner work help twin flames gain insight into their own emotions, triggers, and limitations, and create space for healing and growth.

By prioritizing self-love and healing, twin flames create a strong foundation for their relationship. They become more resilient, emotionally available, and capable of navigating the challenges that may arise. Self-love and healing support individual growth and contribute to the overall harmony and evolution of the twin flame connection.

THE GIFT OF SEPARATION

Exploring the purpose and meaning of physical or energetic separation from the twin flame.
The Gift of Separation refers to the period of physical, emotional, or energetic separation between twin flames. It is often seen as a challenging and transformative phase in the twin flame journey, but it also carries significant lessons and opportunities for growth. Here are some aspects of The Gift of Separation:

1. Individual Growth: The Gift of Separation provides an opportunity for individual growth and self-discovery. During this time, twin flames are encouraged to focus on their own personal development, healing, and self-reflection. It allows them to cultivate self-love,

strengthen their sense of self, and pursue their own passions and purpose.

2. Healing and Self-Healing: The period of separation can be a catalyst for deep healing and self-healing. Twin flames may have unresolved emotional wounds or past traumas that need attention and healing. The space created by separation allows them to dive into their own healing journey, addressing their individual wounds and finding inner balance and wholeness.

3. Independence and Self-Reliance: The Gift of Separation encourages twin flames to develop a sense of independence and self-reliance. It invites them to rely on their own inner strength, wisdom, and resources. By cultivating self-reliance, twin flames learn to trust in their own abilities and develop a solid foundation of self-worth.

4. Surrender and Divine Timing: The period of separation often teaches twin flames the importance of surrendering to the divine timing of their connection. It helps them release attachment to specific outcomes or expectations and trust that everything is unfolding according to a higher plan. It fosters surrendering to the journey itself and embracing the lessons and growth that come with it.

5. Union Preparation: The Gift of Separation serves as a preparation phase for the eventual reunion and union of twin flames. It allows both individuals to work on themselves, clear any energetic or emotional blockages, and align with their higher selves. The separation period can help them become more ready and aligned for a harmonious and balanced union when the time is right.

6. Spiritual Connection: Despite the physical separation, twin flames often maintain a strong spiritual connection during this phase. They may experience telepathic communication, synchronicities, or a heightened sense of intuition. This spiritual connection serves as a reminder of the deeper bond they share and keeps them connected on a higher level.

It's important to note that the duration and intensity of the separation phase can vary for each twin flame pair. While it can be a challenging and painful time, it is ultimately seen as a gift because of the growth, healing, and self-discovery it facilitates. The Gift of Separation teaches twin flames important lessons about self-love, surrender, and personal evolution, preparing them for a deeper union when the timing is aligned.

EMBRACING INDIVIDUAL PATHS

Navigating the process of individuation, self-discovery, and aligning with one's life purpose.

Embracing individual paths refers to recognizing and honouring the unique journeys and personal growth of each twin flame separately. It involves acknowledging that while twin flames share a deep spiritual connection and are destined to come together, they also have their own individual paths to walk.

Here are some key aspects of embracing individual:

1. Self-Discovery and Personal Growth: Each twin flame is on their own path of self-discovery and personal growth. Embracing individual paths means allowing each person to explore their own passions, interests, and purpose. It involves supporting and encouraging the individual growth of each twin

flame, understanding that their personal journeys contribute to the wholeness and authenticity they bring to the union.

2. Autonomy and Independence: Embracing individual paths involves recognizing and respecting each twin flame's autonomy and independence. It means honouring their freedom to make choices, pursue their own dreams, and follow their own intuition. It requires trusting that each person knows what is best for their own journey and allowing them the space to navigate it accordingly.

3. Respecting Differences and Timing: Embracing individual paths also entails respecting the differences in experiences, timing, and lessons between twin flames. It acknowledges that each person may be at a different stage of their journey and may require different

experiences and lessons to facilitate their growth. This understanding helps foster patience, compassion, and acceptance in the twin flame connection.

4. Healing and Self-Care: Embracing individual paths recognizes the importance of individual healing and self-care. It means honouring the need for each twin flame to prioritize their own well-being and take the necessary steps for healing and personal growth. This allows each person to show up as their best and most authentic selves in the twin flame union.

5. Collaboration and Support: While twin flames have individual paths, embracing them doesn't mean completely disconnecting from each other. It involves finding a balance between individuality and collaboration. Twin flames can support and uplift each other as

they navigate their own journeys, offering guidance, encouragement, and love.

6. Trusting the Divine Plan: Embracing individual paths ultimately requires trusting the divine plan and the higher wisdom behind the twin flame connection. It involves surrendering to the greater purpose and timing of the union, knowing that each twin flame's individual path is ultimately aligned with the highest good of both individuals and the union itself.

By embracing individual paths, twin flames honour the individuality, growth, and autonomy of each person. It allows them to support and encourage each other's personal journeys while maintaining a deep and sacred connection. Embracing individual paths ultimately contributes to the strength, authenticity, and harmony of the twin flame union.

CHAPTER 5

REUNION IN HIGHER CONSCIOUSNESS

UNION BEYOND PHYSICALITY

Expanding the concept of twin flame union to encompass a higher level of consciousness and unity.
Union beyond refers to a deep, spiritual connection that transcends physical proximity or presence. It is an understanding that the bond between twin

flames goes beyond the physical realm and is based on a profound soul connection. Here are some key aspects of union beyond physicality:

1. Soul Connection: Twin flames share a soul connection that goes beyond the physical realm. It is a connection at the soul level, where their energies and essences intertwine. This connection remains strong regardless of physical distance or separation.

2. Energetic and Spiritual Union: Union beyond physicality emphasizes the energetic and spiritual aspect of the twin flame connection. It is about the merging of souls, hearts, and minds on a deep energetic level, regardless of physical presence. Twin flames can feel each other's energy, communicate telepathically, and experience a profound sense of unity even when physically apart.

3. Unconditional Love: Union beyond physicality is grounded in unconditional love. Twin flames have a deep and unwavering love for each other that goes beyond physical attraction or external circumstances. It is a love that is pure, accepting, and transcends any limitations imposed by the physical world.

4. Connection through Time and Space: The spiritual connection between twin flames allows them to transcend the constraints of time and space. They can feel connected to each other even when physically separated by distance or time. The bond between twin flames remains strong and can be felt across various dimensions and lifetimes.

5. Inner Alignment: Union beyond physicality emphasizes the importance of inner alignment and spiritual growth. Each twin flame is

encouraged to focus on their own spiritual development and inner transformation. By aligning with their higher selves and embracing their own spiritual path, they contribute to the depth and strength of the spiritual union with their twin flame.

6. Divine Timing: Union beyond physicality acknowledges the role of divine timing in the twin flame journey. It is an understanding that the timing of physical union may not always align with the spiritual connection. Twin flames trust that the universe has a greater plan and that the timing of their physical reunion will unfold according to divine guidance.

Union beyond physicality is a profound aspect of the twin flame connection. It invites twin flames to recognize and embrace the depth of their spiritual bond and to prioritize spiritual growth, inner alignment, and unconditional love. By acknowledging and nurturing this union beyond the physical realm, twin flames can strengthen their connection and deepen their spiritual journey together.

INTEGRATION AND BALANCE

Exploring the importance of integrating lessons learned and achieving balance within oneself.

Integration and refer to the process of harmonizing and merging various aspects of oneself and the twin flame connection. It involves embracing both the light and shadow aspects, integrating the spiritual and physical realms, and finding equilibrium within the dynamic nature of the relationship.

Integration: Integration is about bringing together different aspects of oneself, including the mind, body, heart, and soul. It entails embracing all experiences, emotions, and lessons, and integrating them into one's being. In the twin flame journey, integration involves recognizing and accepting both the positive and challenging aspects of the connection, as well as integrating the lessons learned from the experiences.

Balance: Balance refers to finding equilibrium and harmony within oneself and the twin flame relationship. It involves maintaining a sense of stability and centeredness amidst the intense energy and emotional fluctuations that can arise. Balancing the energies between twin flames allows for a healthy and sustainable connection that honours the individuality and mutual growth of both partners.

Integration and balance require self-awareness, self-reflection, and a commitment to personal growth. It involves embracing one's own strengths and weaknesses, understanding triggers and patterns, and cultivating self-love and self-care. It also involves recognizing the needs and perspectives of the twin flame counterpart and fostering open communication and mutual support.

By integrating and balancing various aspects within oneself and the twin flame relationship, individuals can find a sense of wholeness and completeness. It allows for the harmonious blending of energies and a deeper connection that is rooted in understanding, acceptance, and mutual growth. Integration and balance contribute to the overall evolution and spiritual expansion of both individuals on their twin flame journey.

Printed in Great Britain
by Amazon